AUSTRALIA'S SCARIEST CREATURES

BY JOHN LESLEY

FIERCE REPTILES

REDBACK publishing

First published 2024 by
Redback Publishing
PO Box 357 Frenchs Forest NSW 2086
Australia

www.redbackpublishing.com
orders@redbackpublishing.com

ISBN 978-1-761400-42-1 HBK

Author: John Lesley
Editor: Caroline Thomas
Designer: Redback Publishing
Original illustrations © Redback Publishing 2024
Originated by Redback Publishing

Acknowledgements
Abbreviations: l—left, r—right, b—bottom, t—top, c—centre, m—middle
We would like to thank the following for permission to reproduce photographs (images © Shutterstock unless otherwise stated)

Disclaimer
Every effort has been made to contact copyright holders of any material reproduced in this book. Any omissions will be rectified in subsequent printings if notice is given to the publisher.

NATIONAL LIBRARY OF AUSTRALIA
A catalogue record for this book is available from the National Library of Australia

CONTENTS

PERENTIE

Varanus giganteus

Although perenties can grow to over two metres long, they are not nearly as well known in Australia as their distant reptilian cousins, the crocodiles. Perenties are monitor lizards and are a type of goanna. They have been on Earth for many millions of years and are one of the biggest lizards found anywhere.

LIFECYCLE

Perenties live alone and only come together to mate. The female lays about ten eggs in the sandy soil or sometimes directly into a termite nest. The eggs take many months to hatch.

HABITAT

In the arid regions where it is most often found, the perentie digs a burrow for shelter, using its very large and strong claws. They also live amongst rocks or in small caves. The claws are useful when they climb trees in search of birds and eggs.

FOOD

Perenties are carnivores. They can run extremely fast when hunting their prey, which they then bite and shake. They eat any small animals they come across, including lizards, mammals and birds.

FACT

The perentie is one of the biggest lizards in the world and is Australia's largest lizard.

FACT

The perentie is related to Indonesia's fearsome and huge Komodo dragon.

The forked tongue flicks constantly in and out to get information from scent particles in the air.

FACT FILE

Length: up to 2 metres
Colour: sandy or grey with camouflaging dark lines and spots
Venomous: mildly venomous
Habitat: desert and semi-arid regions of Australia
Life span: in captivity, over 10 years
Scientific name: *Varanus giganteus*

CONSERVATION

The perentie has been a traditional food source and special animal for the Indigenous Australian people for many thousands of years. Its numbers in the wild are probably stable, but it is so rarely seen that its conservation status is not entirely certain. Dingoes, eagles and other perenties are their predators, and perenties will use their teeth, claws and thrashing tail for defence against them.

VENOM AND BITING

Since it lives in parts of Australia where the human population is low, encounters between perenties and people are rare. If it feels under threat, a perentie may hiss and jump forwards. Sometimes they stand up on their back legs to look bigger. People bitten by a perentie may suffer from the effects of the venom, as well as receiving a dangerous dose of bacteria into the wound.

GOANNA

Varanes

Australians are used to seeing large goannas in bushland and deserts. Goannas grow to about a metre in length, and walk with a side-to-side style, like a crocodile. Some goannas are very good at climbing high into gum trees, where they steal eggs and baby birds. If you surprise a goanna on the ground, it will flatten itself and may stand up on its back legs, in an attempt to look bigger and more scary. Get too close and watch out! They bite!

LIFECYCLE

The female goanna lays her eggs in a burrow that she digs in the ground using her long, strong claws. Some goannas lay their eggs inside termite nests. The adults can live for thirty years or more.

HABITAT

Goannas live in bushland, deserts and open grassland. Like all lizards, they don't like cold weather, since they need the heat from the Sun to give them enough energy to move around.

FOOD

Goannas are carnivores. They hunt for birds, frogs, small lizards and mammals. They can smell a dead animal a long distance away, using scent receptors in their forked tongue. Farmers will often see goannas feeding on dead sheep or cows.

FACT

Goannas can stand up and run on their back legs!

FACT

40,000 years ago, goannas of up to six metres long roamed Australia!

If a goanna bites you, it won't let go!

FACT FILE

Length: about 1 metre
Colour: mottled brown, black or sandy colours
Venomous: yes
Habitat: bush, grassland and arid regions
Life span: about 30 years
Scientific name: *Varanes*

FACT

Over a hundred years ago, an ointment made from goanna fat promised it could cure infections!

CONSERVATION

There are over twenty types of goannas in Australia, ranging in length from twenty centimetres to a metre. They are under threat from loss of habitat, being squashed by cars on roads, and being eaten by feral animals such as cats and dogs.

VENOM AND BITING

Goannas have sharp teeth and will hold on tightly if they bite you. Attacks on children generally result in painful wounds, usually on hands and feet. Goannas have venom as well as lots of bacteria in their mouth, which means their bite wounds can take a long time to heal. A scared goanna will run at a human or a tree to escape, so don't get too close, and never try to feed them.

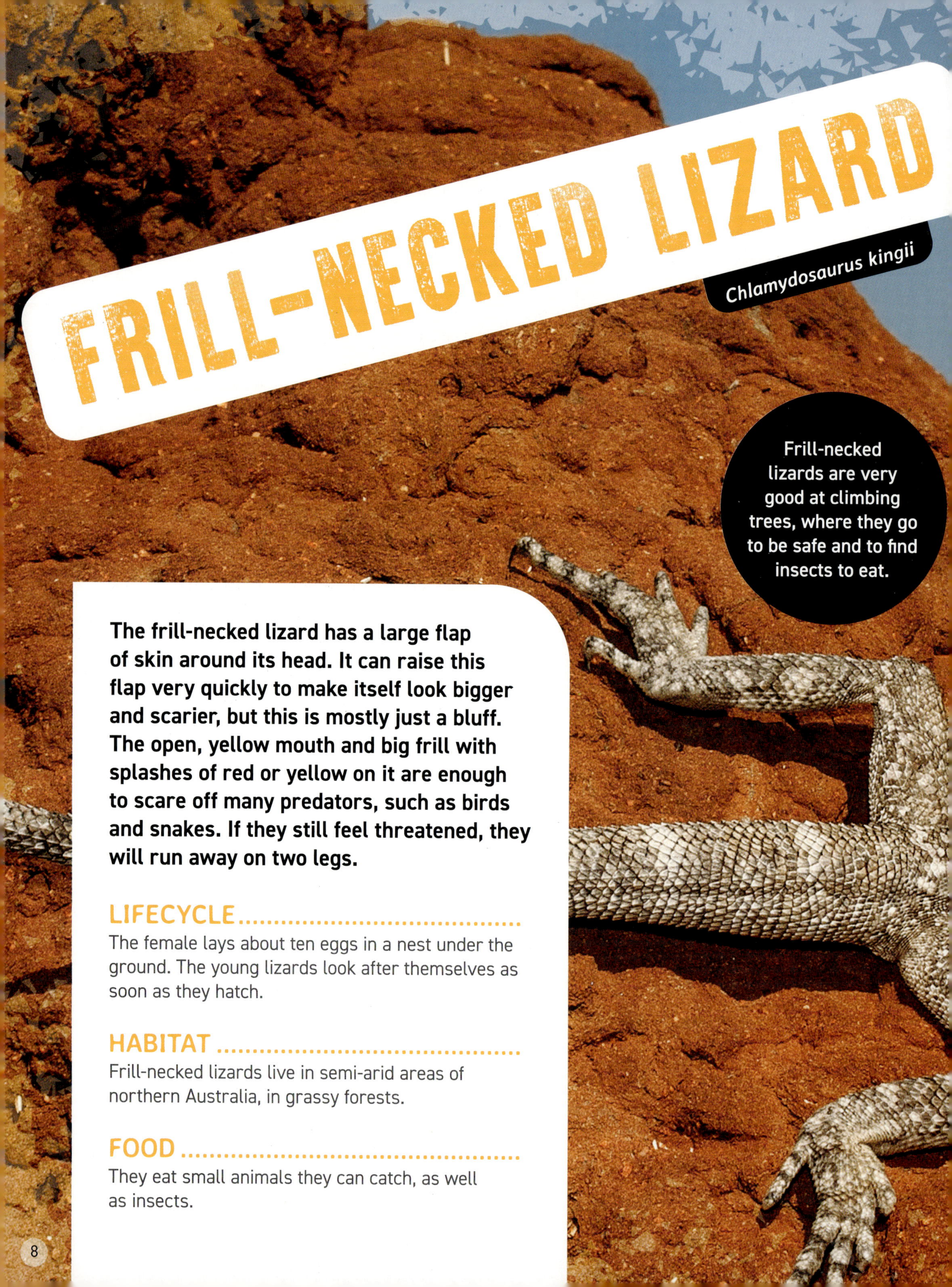

FRILL-NECKED LIZARD

Chlamydosaurus kingii

Frill-necked lizards are very good at climbing trees, where they go to be safe and to find insects to eat.

The frill-necked lizard has a large flap of skin around its head. It can raise this flap very quickly to make itself look bigger and scarier, but this is mostly just a bluff. The open, yellow mouth and big frill with splashes of red or yellow on it are enough to scare off many predators, such as birds and snakes. If they still feel threatened, they will run away on two legs.

LIFECYCLE

The female lays about ten eggs in a nest under the ground. The young lizards look after themselves as soon as they hatch.

HABITAT

Frill-necked lizards live in semi-arid areas of northern Australia, in grassy forests.

FOOD

They eat small animals they can catch, as well as insects.

FACT

Males fight each other by biting and showing off their frills.

FACT FILE

Length: 50 centimetres to 1 metre, including tail
Colour: mottled brown, grey and sandy scales
Venomous: no
Habitat: semi-arid areas of Australia with open forests
Life span: about 10 years in the wild
Scientific name: *Chlamydosaurus kingii*

CONSERVATION

Because it lives in remote areas, the frill-necked lizard is not under threat of extinction at present.

VENOM AND BITING

Frill-necked lizards do not have venom, but they will bite you if you threaten them. They have very sharp teeth.

CROCODILE

Crocodylus

There are two types of crocodile in Australia, the 'salties' and the 'freshies'. Salties live in seawater near the shore, and in rivers that have tidal flows from the sea. Freshies live in freshwater. No waterway in Australia's Top End is completely safe for swimming, and there are signs everywhere telling people to beware of crocodiles.

LIFECYCLE

The female crocodile lays eggs in a nest beside the water. She usually guards the nest until the babies hatch.

HABITAT

The huge and dangerous crocodile is found in waterways across the northern parts of Australia. They need to live in hot climates since they rely on the heat from the environment to give them enough energy to move and hunt.

FACT

Cassius is a male saltwater croc living in captivity on Green Island in the Great Barrier Reef.

He is over 120 years old!

In some parts of Australia's north, there are as many crocs as humans!

FACT FILE

Length: between 3 and 6 metres, including tail
Colour: dark, mottled browns and greys
Venomous: no
Habitat: fresh and salty water, and land nearby
Life span: up to 70 years
Scientific name:
Crocodylus johnstoni (freshwater croc)
Crocodylus porosus (saltwater croc)
People killed each year: 1 or 2 deaths every couple of years

FACT

AS OLD AS DINOSAURS

Saltwater crocodiles are one of the oldest creatures walking the planet.

FOOD

Crocodiles are carnivores, which means they eat meat. They hunt animals by lying still under the water and waiting for prey to come to them. They will grab prey in the water, from the edge of a river or lake, or off a beach.

CONSERVATION

Before conservation measures were put in place in the 1970s, crocodile numbers in Australia had diminished to only a few thousand. They are now safe from extinction.

VENOM AND BITING

Crocodiles do not have venom, but their bite can be lethal. To kill their prey, they bite them and then may drag them under the water to drown.

TURTLES AND TORTOISES

Turtles and tortoises are reptiles. Their shell is a part of their spine, and it is an adaptation to help protect them from predators.

Sea turtles live in water most of the time, and they have evolved to have flippers and webbed feet. These turtles need to come onto land to lay their eggs.

Freshwater turtles live on land and in creeks and lakes in a variety of habitats, including forests, grassland and deserts.

FACT

Australia does not have any native, land-based tortoises.

FRESHWATER TURTLES IN AUSTRALIA

Eastern long-necked turtle
Northern snake-necked turtle
Pig-nosed turtle
Bellinger River turtle
Murray River turtle
Mary River turtle
Manning River turtle

In Australia, freshwater turtles are often referred to as tortoises.

SEA TURTLES IN AUSTRALIAN WATERS

Flatback sea turtle
Loggerhead sea turtle
Green sea turtle
Hawksbill sea turtle
Leatherback sea turtle

THORNY DEVIL

Moloch horridus

FACT

A thorny devil has a lump that looks like a second head on the back of its neck. This is probably used to confuse predators.

The thorny devil lizard is completely covered in large thorn-like spikes. These spikes have two important purposes. They protect the lizard from attack, but they also channel drops of dew down to the mouth. This is often the only water source these lizards have in their desert environment.

LIFECYCLE

The female lays about ten eggs in a burrow. They hatch after about three months.

HABTAT

Thorny devils live in desert habitats, where their sandy colours help to camouflage them from predators.

FOOD

Thorny devils eat ants. This single food source makes thorny devils vulnerable to any change in their habitat that would affect the ant population.

CONSERVATION

Thorny devils are not presently under any threat of extinction, largely due to living in isolated, desert regions.

FACT

They can eat 3,000 ants in one meal.

If you have only ever seen photos of thorny devils, you may be surprised to see that a real one is quite small, only about twenty centimetres long.

FACT FILE

Length: about 20 centimetres including the tail
Colour: yellow, brown and orange
Habitat: deserts
Life span: over 10 years
Scientific name: *Moloch horridus*

EASTERN WATER DRAGON

Intellagama lesueurii

The eastern water dragon is commonly seen in bushland near Sydney. They have a large head and strong, sharp claws.

LIFECYCLE

Water dragon females lay about ten eggs in soft soil. After hatching, the young have to be quick to avoid being eaten by older water dragons.

HABITAT

The eastern water dragon lives in bushland along the eastern, forested parts of Australia.

FOOD

Water dragons are omnivores, eating plants, animals and insects. They have been seen taking food such as bread from people. This is not good for them. Never give this food to a reptile. In fact, avoid feeding wild animals, as this can make them extremely sick, even though they seem to like eating human food.

FACT

Tame water dragons sometimes demand food from people in restaurants located next to bushland areas – a frightening experience for someone who has never had a metre-long lizard run up to them!

In an attempt to look scary, a water dragon will stand up on its back legs.

FACT FILE

Length: about 1 metre
Colour: grey body with dark grey bands
Venomous: no
Habitat: in and near fresh water, and in trees
Life span: over 20 years
Scientific name: *Intellagama lesueurii*

CONSERVATION ...

Water dragons can become threatened if they lose their habitat when bushland is cleared for housing and farmland. The creeks they rely on may become polluted or enclosed as drains under roads.

VENOM AND BITING ....

Like most lizards, water dragons will bite if annoyed. Their bite is not known to be venomous.

SNAKES

Snakes are reptiles that have lost their legs. This adaptation enables them to hide in narrow areas between rocks. Not having legs does not stop snakes from climbing trees or getting up into the roofs of houses.

LIFECYCLE

Snakes lay soft eggs. After hatching, the young snakes are usually able to look after themselves right away. Some snakes can live for twenty years.

HABITAT

In Australia, snakes live in most habitats, including rainforests, grassland, in fresh water and in the sea, on farmland and in deserts. Some snakes are very happy living near houses and towns, where they feed on the rats and mice that also like to live near humans.

FOOD

Snakes are carnivores. They hunt their prey and swallow it whole. Some snakes inject venom into their prey before eating it. Pythons do not have venom, but they crush their prey to kill it before swallowing it.

CONSERVATION

Some types of snake are under threat of extinction, while others are thriving.

VENOM AND BITING

Some snakes have venom, and they bite. Their venom can be deadly to humans.

SOME OF AUSTRALIA'S MANY SNAKES
COPPERHEAD
GREEN TREE PYTHON
SEA SNAKES
CHILDREN'S PYTHON
DEATH ADDER
BLIND SNAKE
TAIPAN
TIGER SNAKE
DIAMOND PYTHONS
RED-BELLIED BLACK SNAKE

HOW ARE REPTILES SPECIAL?

Reptiles mostly lay eggs, although some produce live young that are ready to run off and look after themselves soon after birth

Some reptiles are highly intelligent and are even able to count

Reptile eggs usually have soft shells, making them less likely to crack when they are buried in underground nests

Snakes are reptiles that have lost their legs

They are cold-blooded, which means they need the heat from the Sun or their surroundings to become warm enough to move around

Reptiles have scales that give them a strong outer covering

The scaly skin is shed in sheets so that the reptile can grow bigger

Reptiles mostly have claws and sharp teeth

MORE AUSTRALIAN REPTILES

CENTRAL NETTLED DRAGON
MARY RIVER TURTLE
EASTERN LONG-NECKED TURTLE
GREEN TURTLE
BEARDED DRAGON
LACE MONITOR

WORLD'S MOST SCARY REPTILES

PERENTIE - AUSTRALIA

RED-BELLIED BLACK SNAKE - AUSTRALIA

RATTLESNAKE - NORTH AND SOUTH AMERICA

KOMODO DRAGON - INDONESIA

KING COBRA - ASIA

GILA MONSTER - USA AND MEXICO

ANACONDA - SOUTH AMERICA

The scariest reptile that ever lived was probably the *T. rex*.

Fortunately, we are separated from it by many millions of years!

SALTWATER CROCODILE - AUSTRALIA

ALLIGATOR SNAPPING TURTLE - USA

ARE THEY DINOSAURS?

QUESTION & ANSWER

Were the dinosaurs just like today's reptiles, only bigger?

A: Although the dinosaurs were reptiles, they had some interesting features that modern reptiles do not have:

- Some dinosaurs had feathers
- Dinosaurs may have been able to control their body temperature. This would have given them the energy to move around, without relying on heat from the Sun

?

QUESTION & ANSWER

? Are all reptiles descended from dinosaurs?

A: No! Dinosaurs existed at the same time as the ancestors of crocodiles, snakes and lizards. They all lived on Earth at the same time, millions of years ago, but each evolved into different types of animals that are alive today. The dinosaurs seem to have been the ancestors of modern birds, not of lizards, snakes or crocodiles.

? Were the dinosaurs reptiles?

A: Yes! Dinosaurs were reptiles.

REPTILES AS A PETS

FEAR!

Reptiles are not for people who want a friendly pet that likes to cuddle!

In Australia, all native reptiles are protected animals, which means that they cannot be removed from or released into the bush. Killing any native animal is also unlawful.

Laws for keeping reptiles as pets vary in each State and Territory. Those that do allow keeping a native reptile sometimes insist that it is obtained from a licensed dealer. You may need to apply for your own reptile licence as well. In New South Wales, snakes from other countries cannot be kept as pets.

FEAR!

Some people love to keep a pet that scares all their friends.

FACT

A pet snake can escape from its enclosure by pushing itself through any gap.

LACE MONITOR

VICTORIA, AUSTRALIA

THORNY DEVIL

DESERT PLANT

ROUGH-SCALED SNAKE

GLOSSARY

Reptile Word List

ancestors	living things in the past from which modern life has come
billabong	lake left behind when a river changes its course
bluff	pretence
burrow	hole in the ground that is an animal's home
camouflage	outer covering that hides an animal
carnivore	animal that eats meat
dew	water droplets that form out of the air
evolve	change over time
extinction	when all animals of one type are dead
forked	split into two parts
isolated	not being near other things
omnivore	animal that eats both meat and plants
semi-arid	area with low rainfall, often on the edge of a desert
stable	steady and not changing
thriving	growing well and reproducing
venom	poison produced by an animal to kill prey or defend itself
webbed feet	having skin between the toes

FRESHWATER CROCODILE FOOT

INDEX